NURSERY RHYMES

Mother Goose

MOTHER GOOSE RHYMES

Counting Your Way

NUMBER NURSERY RHYMES

compiled by Terry Pierce
illustrated by Andrea Petrlik Huseinovic

PICTURE WINDOW BOOKS
Minneapolis, Minnesota

Special thanks to our advisers for their expertise:

Terry Flaherty, Ph.D., Professor of English
Minnesota State University, Mankato

Susan Kesselring, M.A., Literacy Educator
Rosemount–Apple Valley–Eagan (Minnesota) School District

Editors: Christianne Jones and Dodie Marie Miller
Designer: Tracy Davies
Page Production: Angela Kilmer
Art Director: Nathan Gassman
The illustrations in this book were created with acrylics.

Editor's Note: Editorial and formatting decisions for most of
the nursery rhymes in this book were based on the following
source: *The Random House Book of Mother Goose* (1986),
selected and illustrated by Arnold Lobel.

Picture Window Books
5115 Excelsior Boulevard
Suite 232
Minneapolis, MN 55416
877-845-8392
www.picturewindowbooks.com

Library of Congress Cataloging-in-Publication Data
Pierce, Terry.
Counting your way : number nursery rhymes / compiled by
Terry Pierce ; illustrated by Andrea Petrlik Huseinovic
p. cm. — (Mother Goose rhymes)
Summary: An illustrated collection of twenty nursery rhymes
featuring numbers.
ISBN-13: 978-1-4048-2346-4 (library binding)
ISBN-10: 1-4048-2346-8 (library binding)
ISBN-13: 978-1-4048-2352-5 (paperback)
ISBN-10: 1-4048-2352-2 (paperback)
1. Nursery rhymes. 2. Numerals—Juvenile poetry.
3. Children's poetry. [1. Nursery rhymes. 2. Numerals—
Poetry.] I. Huseinovic, Andrea Petrlik, 1966- ill. II. Mother
Goose. Selections. III. Title. IV. Title: Number nursery rhymes.
PZ8.3.P558643Cou 2006
398.8—dc22 [E]   2006027241

TABLE OF CONTENTS

MOTHER GOO

NURSERY RHYMES ABOUT NUMBERS

Do you like numbers? NUMBERS are FUN, especially when you can say them in rhyme. Hundreds of years ago, people made up nursery rhymes with numbers and counting riddles. See how many number words you can find in these rhymes.

ONE, TWO, BUCKLE MY SHOE

One, two, buckle my shoe;

Three, four, open the door;

Five, six, pick up sticks;

Seven, eight, lay them straight;

Nine, ten, a big fat hen;

Eleven, twelve, I hope you're well;

Thirteen, fourteen, draw the curtain;

Fifteen, sixteen, the maids in the kitchen;

Seventeen, eighteen, she's in waiting;

Nineteen, twenty, my stomach's empty.

Please, ma'am, to give me some dinner.

BAA, BAA, BLACK SHEEP

Baa, baa, black sheep,
Have you any wool?
Yes, sir, yes, sir,
Three bags full,
One for the master,
One for the dame,
One for the little boy
Who lives in the lane.

RUB-A-DUB-DUB

Rub-a-dub-dub,

Three men in a tub,

And who do you think they be?

The butcher, the baker, the candlestick maker,

Turn them out, knaves all three.

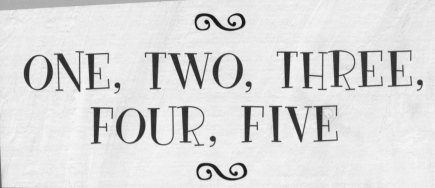

ONE, TWO, THREE, FOUR, FIVE

One, two, three, four, five,

Once I caught a fish alive.

Six, seven, eight, nine, ten,

Then I let it go again.

Why did you let it go?

Because it bit my finger so.

Which finger did it bite?

The little finger on the right.

ONE FOR THE MONEY

One for the money,
And two for the show,
Three to make ready,
And four to go.

SING A SONG OF SIXPENCE

Sing a song of sixpence,
A pocket full of rye;
Four and twenty blackbirds
Baked in a pie.

When the pie was opened
The birds began to sing;
Was not that a dainty dish
To set before the king?

The king was in his counting house,
Counting out his money;
The queen was in the parlor
Eating bread and honey.

The maid was in the garden
Hanging out the clothes;
Along came a blackbird
And pecked off her nose.

ST. IVES

As I was going to St. Ives,
I met a man with seven wives.
Each wife had seven sacks,
Each sack had seven cats,
Each cat had seven kits;
Kits, cats, sacks, and wives,
How many were going to St. Ives?

THREE WISE MEN OF GOTHAM

Three wise men of Gotham,

They went to sea in a bowl,

And if the bowl had been stronger,

My song would have been longer.

PAIRS OR PEARS

Twelve pairs were hanging high,

Twelve knights came riding by,

Each knight took a pear,

And left a dozen hanging there.

ONE, TWO, THREE, FOUR

One, two, three, four,

Mary's at the cottage door.

Five, six, seven, eight,

Eating cherries off a plate.

18

I LOVE SIXPENCE

I love sixpence, jolly, jolly sixpence,
I love sixpence as my life.
I spent a penny of it, I spent a penny of it,
I took a penny home to my wife.

I love fourpence, jolly, jolly fourpence,
I love fourpence as my life.
I spent twopence of it, I spent twopence of it,
I took twopence home to my wife.

I have nothing, jolly, jolly nothing,
I love nothing as my life.
I spent nothing of it, I spent nothing of it,
I took nothing home to my wife.

miss one, TWO, AND THREE

Miss One, Two, and Three

Could never agree

While they gossiped around

A tea-caddy.

ONE, TWO, THREE

...d Billy loves tea,
How good you be,
One, two, three,
I love coffee,
And Billy loves tea.

GREGORY GRIGGS

Gregory Griggs, Gregory Griggs,

Had twenty-seven different wigs.

He wore them up, he wore them down,

To please the people of the town.

He wore them east, he wore them west,

And never could tell which one he liked best.

THREE YOUNG RATS WITH BLACK FELT HATS

Three young rats with black felt hats,
Three young ducks with white straw flats,
Three young dogs with curling tails,
Three young cats with demi-veils,
Went out to walk with two young pigs
In satin vests and sorrel wigs.
But suddenly it chanced to rain
And so they all went home again.

THERE WERE TWO WRENS

There were two wrens upon a tree,

Whistle and I'll come to thee;

Another came, and then there were three,

Whistle and I'll come to thee;

Another came and there were four.

You needn't whistle anymore,

For being frightened, off they flew,

And there are none to show to you.

MRS. HEN

Chook, chook, chook, chook, chook,

Good morning, Mrs. Hen.

How many chickens have you got?

Madam, I've got ten.

Four of them are yellow,

And four of them are brown,

And two of them are speckled red,

The nicest in town.

26

I BOUGHT A DOZEN NEW-LAID EGGS

I bought a dozen new-laid eggs

Of good old Farmer Dickens;

I hobbled home upon two legs

And found them full of chickens.

THE GALLANT SHIP

Three times round goes our gallant ship,
And three times round goes she,
Three times round goes our gallant ship,
And sinks to the bottom of the sea.

Magpie, magpie, flutter and flee,

Turn up your tail and good luck come to me.

One for sorrow, two for joy,

Three for a girl, four for a boy,

Five for silver, six for gold,

Seven for a secret ne'er to be told.

THE HISTORY OF NURSERY RHYMES AND
MOTHER GOOSE

Nursery rhymes circulated orally for hundreds of years. In the 18th century, collectors wrote down the rhymes, printed them, and sold them to parents and other adults to help them remember the rhymes so they could share them with children.

Some of these collections were called "Mother Goose" collections. Nobody knows exactly who Mother Goose was (though there are plenty of myths about her), but she was probably a respected storyteller. Occasionally the rhymes commented on real people and events. The meaning of many of the rhymes has been lost, but the catchy rhythms remain.

Mother Goose nursery rhymes have evolved from many sources through time. From the 1600s until now, the appealing rhythms, rhymes, humor, and playfulness found in these verses, stories, and concepts contribute to what readers now know as Mother Goose nursery rhymes.

TO LEARN MORE

AT THE LIBRARY

Brauckmann-Towns, Krista. *Buckle My Shoe and Other Counting Rhymes.* Lincolnwood, Ill.: Publications International, 1996.

Dillon, Leo, and Diane. *Mother Goose Numbers on the Loose.* Orlando: Harcourt, 2007.

Schell, Becky. *Mother Goose From 1-10.* Los Angeles: Price, Stern, Sloan, 1987.

ON THE WEB

FactHound offers a safe, fun way to find Web sites related to this book. All of the sites on FactHound have been researched by our staff.

1. Visit *www.facthound.com*
2. Type in this special code:
   1404823468
3. Click on the FETCH IT button.

Your trusty FactHound will fetch the best sites for you!

INDEX OF FIRST LINES

LOOK FOR ALL OF THE BOOKS IN THE MOTHER GOOSE RHYMES SERIES:

Counting Your Way: Number Nursery Rhymes
Cuddly Critters: Animal Nursery Rhymes
Forecasting Fun: Weather Nursery Rhymes
Friendly Faces: People Nursery Rhymes
Sleepytime: Bedtime Nursery Rhymes
Ticktock: Time Nursery Rhymes

Mother Goose

NURSERY RHYMES